THE STORY OF THE
NEW YORK KNICKS

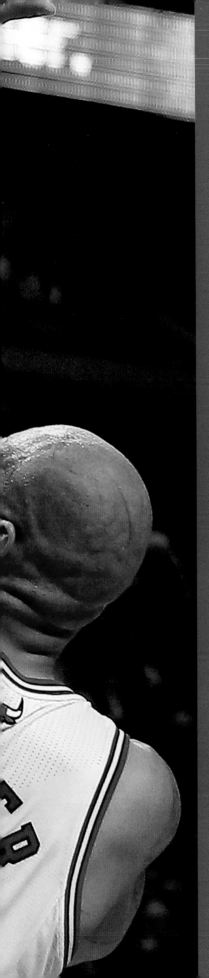

THE NBA:
A HISTORY
OF HOOPS

THE STORY OF THE
NEW YORK
KNICKS

SHANE FREDERICK

CREATIVE
PAPER BACKS

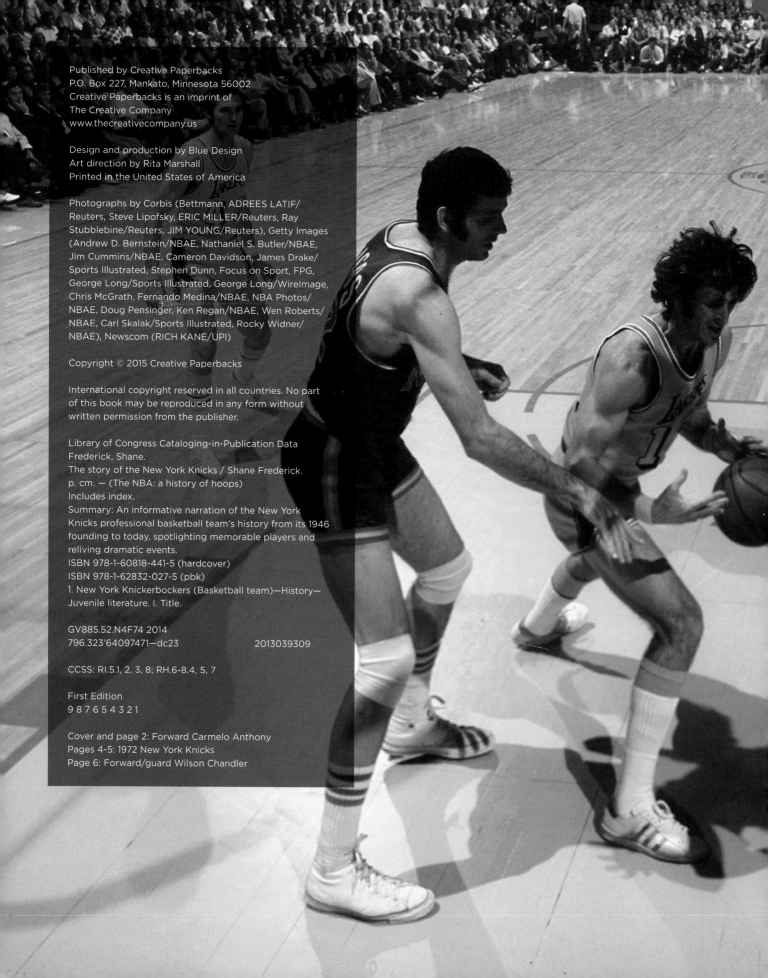

Published by Creative Paperbacks
P.O. Box 227, Mankato, Minnesota 56002
Creative Paperbacks is an imprint of
The Creative Company
www.thecreativecompany.us

Design and production by Blue Design
Art direction by Rita Marshall
Printed in the United States of America

Photographs by Corbis (Bettmann, ADREES LATIF/
Reuters, Steve Lipofsky, ERIC MILLER/Reuters, Ray
Stubblebine/Reuters, JIM YOUNG/Reuters), Getty Images
(Andrew D. Bernstein/NBAE, Nathaniel S. Butler/NBAE,
Jim Cummins/NBAE, Cameron Davidson, James Drake/
Sports Illustrated, Stephen Dunn, Focus on Sport, FPG,
George Long/Sports Illustrated, George Long/WireImage,
Chris McGrath, Fernando Medina/NBAE, NBA Photos/
NBAE, Doug Pensinger, Ken Regan/NBAE, Wen Roberts/
NBAE, Carl Skalak/Sports Illustrated, Rocky Widner/
NBAE), Newscom (RICH KANE/UPI)

Library of Congress Cataloging-in-Publication Data
Frederick, Shane.
The story of the New York Knicks / Shane Frederick.
p. cm. — (The NBA: a history of hoops)
Includes index.
Summary: An informative narration of the New York
Knicks professional basketball team's history from its 1946
founding to today, spotlighting memorable players and
reliving dramatic events.
ISBN 978-1-60818-441-5 (hardcover)
ISBN 978-1-62832-027-5 (pbk)
1. New York Knickerbockers (Basketball team)—History—
Juvenile literature. I. Title.

GV885.52.N4F74 2014
796.323'64097471—dc23   2013039309

CCSS: RI.5.1, 2, 3, 8; RH.6-8.4, 5, 7

First Edition
9 8 7 6 5 4 3 2 1

Cover and page 2: Forward Carmelo Anthony
Pages 4-5: 1972 New York Knicks
Page 6: Forward/guard Wilson Chandler

TABLE OF CONTENTS

COURTSIDE STORIES

INTRODUCING...

BIG STAGE

NEW YORK'S FAMOUS MANHATTAN SKYLINE IS PUNCTUATED BY SKYSCRAPERS.

To residents and visitors alike, New York City is known for its shows. The Theater District, which includes the famed Broadway, has more than 40 theaters that entertain millions of people each year with plays, musicals, operas, concerts, and ballets. Not far from the Theater District is another big stage. Madison Square Garden is home to some of the best sporting shows in the city—New York Knicks basketball games—which have been running for nearly 70 years.

In 1946, a professional league called the Basketball Association of America (BAA) was founded, and the New York Knickerbockers were one of its first franchises. The team's name was quickly shortened to "Knicks" by sportswriters to save space in sports-page headlines. The Knicks established a reputation as being one of the classiest teams in the BAA and, later, in the National

Basketball Association (NBA). Ned Irish, the club's founder, had a clear-cut philosophy: "We will create first-class conditions for a first-class team in a first-class city," he declared. Thanks to Irish, the Knicks boasted professional basketball's first training camp, its first athletic trainer, and its most aggressive scouting program. Irish also found a first-class coach to lead his new squad—Joe Lapchick, who left nearby St. John's University to take over the local pro team.

Lapchick's reputation as a basketball mentor helped him draw top young talent to the Knicks. In 1947, for example, guard Carl Braun—an outstanding baseball and basketball prospect—decided to break his pitching contract with the New York Yankees for the chance to play basketball under Lapchick. Braun was noted for the deadly accurate two-handed set shot that he released from over his head. He would put up dozens of shots in practice, often whispering "swish" as the ball sailed through the net. A

"SWEETWATER" MAKES HISTORY

In 1950, three years after Jackie Robinson broke Major League Baseball's color barrier, the Knicks became the first NBA team to sign an African American player—forward Nat "Sweetwater" Clifton. The 6-foot-7 Chicago native, whose nickname was derived from his love of soft drinks, had come to the Knicks' attention while performing with the Harlem Globetrotters in the late 1940s. Clifton's huge hands enabled him to snare one-handed rebounds and whip outlet passes to teammates heading downcourt. When he first joined the Knicks, Clifton seemed almost too mild-mannered for New York coach Joe Lapchick. Then, during a preseason game in 1951, a Boston Celtics player shoved Clifton and shouted a racial slur at him. The Knicks forward decked the loudmouthed opponent and offered to take on the entire Boston team. The incident seemed to awaken an aggressive instinct in Clifton and earned him respect around the league. While he was an integral part of the Knicks squad on the court, Clifton was still not allowed to stay at the same hotel as his teammates during road trips to several southern and midwestern cities.

11

The Knicks' first-ever draft pick in 1948, Harry Gallatin was the team's cornerstone for nearly a decade. Gallatin's nickname was "Harry the Horse" because he was so strong. Knicks fans also called him "Mr. Inside" because of his importance to the team near the basket. The 6-foot-6 Gallatin outrebounded players many inches taller than he because, as Knicks forward Vince Boryla noted, "he was simply too stubborn to let an opponent get a rebound." Gallatin led the league in rebounding in 1953–54. Even more impressive was the fact that he never missed a game during his NBA career. In fact, Gallatin often proudly boasted that he had never missed a practice or a game in high school, college, or the pros. A seven-time All-Star during his playing days, Gallatin coached both NBA and college teams following his pro career. He was named NBA Coach of the Year in 1963 when he took the St. Louis Hawks to the Western Division finals. Harry the Horse was inducted into the Basketball Hall of Fame in 1991.

Knicks radio broadcaster overheard the new word and became the first to use it on the air.

While Braun was the team's brightest star, the entire club formed a well-balanced constellation. "Everyone knew his role," said center Harry Gallatin. "Dicky McGuire was the playmaker, Carl [Braun] was the shooter, Ernie Vandeweghe did damage in a kind of all-around way, and Nat [Clifton] and I would sweep the boards, outlet the ball, and run. We played true team ball. Coach Lapchick wouldn't have had it any other way."

apchick's Knicks quickly rose toward the top of the NBA's Eastern Division, even though no starter was taller than 6-foot-6. They relied on crisp passing, strong rebounding, and solid defense. The Knicks were especially tough at playoff time. They reached the division finals four years in a row (1950–53) and played in three straight NBA Finals in 1951, 1952, and 1953. However, the team was never quite able to win a championship.

Then age began to slow down some of the Knicks' best players. Starting with the 1956–57 season, New York finished last in its division 9 out of the next 10 years and made the playoffs just once. Talented players such as forwards Kenny Sears and Willie Naulls and guard Richie Guerin led the Knicks during much of this down period, but they never achieved the expected success as a unit.

Among the retired numbers hanging from the rafters of New York's Madison Square Garden is an unusual banner bearing the name "Holzman" and the number 613. The banner honors William "Red" Holzman, the winningest coach in franchise history, and "613" represents the total number of victories his teams achieved during his 14 seasons as Knicks head coach. When a writer once called Holzman a "genius," the court general gruffly replied, "I don't think there is such a thing as a coaching genius, just a hard worker." Holzman pushed his players hard and demanded that they tame their egos and devote all their energy to playing together as a smooth-running unit. He seldom smiled on the sidelines but almost never raised his voice, either. "Red tries to give one the impression that he's a hard, rough, impersonal coach," said team captain and center Willis Reed. "He's really just a pussycat with more knowledge of basketball than any man I've ever known." During the NBA's 50th anniversary celebration in 1996, Holzman was named one of the league's top 10 coaches of all time.

15

SEEING RED

WILLIS REED BECAME THE FIRST KNICKS PLAYER TO BE NAMED ROOKIE OF THE YEAR.

WILLIS REED

In late 1966, Knicks management, hoping to reverse the team's losing trend, hired William "Red" Holzman as coach. A native New Yorker, Holzman had been an outstanding player in the early days of the NBA, and he had served as the Knicks' top scout for a decade before becoming their coach. Holzman believed strongly that, for a club to win, individuals had to be willing to sacrifice some of their own statistics for the good of the team.

Under Holzman's direction as scout and coach, the Knicks drafted and traded for a remarkable group of team-oriented players. First, there was center Willis Reed, the club's captain and inspirational leader. The 6-foot-9 Reed was wide and strong, and he had the heart to outbattle bigger players. Reed began his Knicks career out of position as a power forward, with 6-foot-11 giant Walt Bellamy as the team's center. However, when Bellamy

17

WILLIS REED

POSITION CENTER
HEIGHT 6-FOOT-9
KNICKS SEASONS
1964–74

Hard work came naturally to Willis Reed. Born in rural Louisiana, Reed began picking cotton at age nine to help support his family. By ninth grade, he split his time among attending high school, playing basketball, and working alongside grown men in a wheat storehouse. Later, at Grambling College, Reed earned a reputation as a tireless rebounder with a soft touch from the outside. The Knicks made him their second pick in the 1964 NBA Draft, and he had an immediate impact, leading the club in scoring and rebounding his rookie year. Reed set many team records during his 10 seasons with the Knicks. He also was named to seven NBA All-Star teams and earned league Most Valuable Player (MVP) honors in 1970. Coach Red Holzman named Reed team captain, and he took the role very seriously, pushing the veterans and encouraging the younger players. "He made you understand that you were very lucky to play in this league," said forward Mel Davis, "but if you worked long and hard on your skills, you would have a prosperous career."

showed little interest in playing defense, Holzman engineered a trade with the Detroit Pistons for forward Dave DeBusschere, an outstanding rebounder and defender. The third frontcourt player was Bill Bradley, who ran tirelessly around the court looking to unleash his deadly outside shot.

The team's starting backcourt consisted of Walt Frazier, a flashy guard who was both an offensive threat and defensive stalwart, and Dick Barnett, an outstanding clutch performer. Coming off the bench were long-range bomber Cazzie Russell and defensive specialist Phil Jackson, a gangly forward who would later become one of the NBA's most successful coaches ever.

olzman molded these individuals into an outstanding two-way unit. "I stressed defense—pressure defense—and team basketball. And, on offense, moving the ball to hit the open man," Holzman explained. Holzman had a somewhat crusty and dictatorial manner, but his players always respected him. "Playing basketball [under Holzman] became more fun than I had ever imagined," said Bradley.

Holzman's team reached its peak in 1969–70, winning a club-record 60 games and storming through the first 2 rounds of the playoffs. For the fourth time in their history, the Knicks prepared to battle for an NBA title. Their opponents were the Los Angeles Lakers, led by future Hall-of-Famers Wilt Chamberlain, Jerry West, and Elgin Baylor. The teams split the first four games, with two going into overtime. New York then won Game 5 but lost Reed when the captain tore a thigh muscle while driving to the basket and had to be carried off the court. With Reed out, Chamberlain easily dominated Game 6, reducing the series to a one-game showdown.

Just before Game 7 began, Reed decided to play despite the pain. He announced the decision to his teammates, who were thrilled. "It was like getting your left arm sewed back on," said Russell. The hometown fans in Madison Square Garden went wild as Reed limped onto the court for the opening tip-off. In their hearts, the game and the championship were already won. Reed scored only four points early in the game, but he played tough defense against Chamberlain. Just having him on the court inspired his teammates and the fans as the Knicks earned a 113–99 victory. Of course, it didn't hurt that Frazier had the game of his life, scoring 36 points and handing out 19 assists. After 23 years, the Knickerbockers were champs at last!

Three years later, the Knicks won a second league title with a slightly different cast. Barnett had been replaced in the starting lineup by high-scoring guard Earl "The Pearl" Monroe, one of the most creative offensive players in NBA history. The Frazier–Monroe backcourt tandem directed another balanced New York attack and propelled the Knicks over the Lakers once again for the 1973 championship.

LIFE BEYOND BASKETBALL

Bill Bradley was a two-time NBA champion with the Knicks. Yet his life's highlights included much more than basketball. Bright and hardworking, Bradley was an Eagle Scout, studied at the prestigious University of Oxford on a Rhodes Scholarship, and served six months in the Air Force Reserve. He also came up with unique workouts to make himself a better athlete, such as putting weights in his shoes and then jumping for extended periods. Only after all that did he suit up for the Knicks for 11 seasons, averaging 12.4 points a game on some star-studded rosters and playing with such savvy and determination that he was later inducted into the Hall of Fame despite his relatively modest statistics. Bradley retired in 1977, but only seven months later, he embarked on a new challenge, winning a seat as a United States senator for the state of New Jersey. Bradley put the same passion that had made him a hoops star into his political career, earning reelection to the Senate twice and even campaigning for the U.S. presidency in 2000.

A PRIZE PICK

BILL "TEACH" CARTWRIGHT USED HIS KNOWLEDGE OF THE GAME TO BETTER THE KNICKS.

ver the next few years, core members of the Knicks' title clubs aged and lost some of their edge. They were replaced by such talented newcomers as guards Ray Williams and Micheal Ray Richardson and center Bill Cartwright, but these new Knicks were unable to match the "team" play of Holzman's champs. After the Knicks stumbled to a 33–49 record in 1981–82, the legendary coach also decided to retire.

Holzman was replaced by Hubie Brown, a demanding leader who required his club to run a patterned offense and press and trap continuously on defense. It took the Knicks players a while to adapt to this new style, but they finally succeeded. One key to their success was the play of forward Bernard King, who arrived in New York in 1982. A fierce competitor, the 6-foot-7 King could score

23

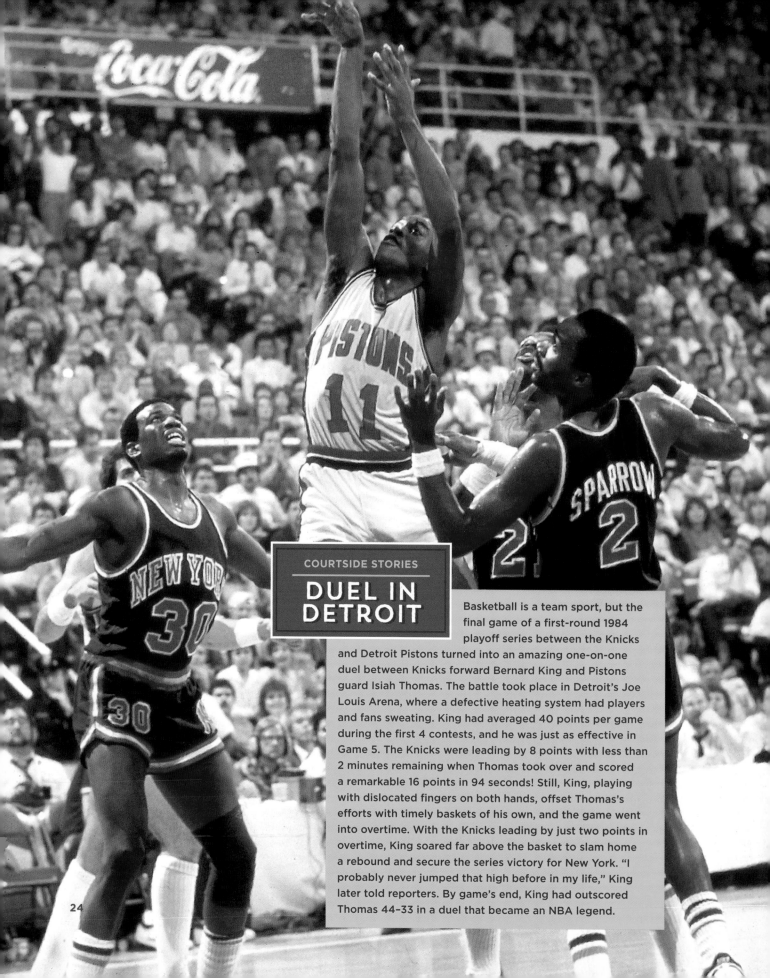

DUEL IN DETROIT

Basketball is a team sport, but the final game of a first-round 1984 playoff series between the Knicks and Detroit Pistons turned into an amazing one-on-one duel between Knicks forward Bernard King and Pistons guard Isiah Thomas. The battle took place in Detroit's Joe Louis Arena, where a defective heating system had players and fans sweating. King had averaged 40 points per game during the first 4 contests, and he was just as effective in Game 5. The Knicks were leading by 8 points with less than 2 minutes remaining when Thomas took over and scored a remarkable 16 points in 94 seconds! Still, King, playing with dislocated fingers on both hands, offset Thomas's efforts with timely baskets of his own, and the game went into overtime. With the Knicks leading by just two points in overtime, King soared far above the basket to slam home a rebound and secure the series victory for New York. "I probably never jumped that high before in my life," King later told reporters. By game's end, King had outscored Thomas 44–33 in a duel that became an NBA legend.

consistently from the outside, but his specialty was driving inside, using his speed and agility to leave defenders behind. "He's like a bird," said Coach Brown. "He swoops toward the basket and seems to be descending. Then, at the last instant, he elevates, and you'll see an incredible move."

King scored nearly 22 points per game in his first season in New York. Then he really found his offensive touch, averaging 26.3 points per game in 1983–84 and leading the NBA with a 32.9 average the next season. Stingy defense and King's scoring propelled the club to the playoffs in both 1983 and 1984. Unfortunately, the Knicks came to rely too heavily on King for their offensive power. When the star forward suffered a devastating knee injury late in the 1984–85 season and was lost for nearly two

JULIUS ERVING (#6) SAID THAT BERNARD KING (#30) WAS HIS "TOUGHEST MATCHUP" EVER.

EARL MONROE

A PERFECT SEVEN

In April 1973, on the way to their second NBA title, the Knicks had one major obstacle to overcome in the Eastern Conference finals—their fiercest rival, the Boston Celtics, winner of 11 league championships. Led by swingman John Havlicek and center Dave Cowens, the Celtics finished far ahead of the Knicks during the regular season and were heavily favored to beat out New York for a spot in the NBA Finals. Unintimidated, the Knicks blew out the Celtics in Game 2 and captured the next two contests to take a commanding three-games-to-one series lead. Then Boston staged exciting fourth-quarter comebacks in Games 5 and 6 to set up a winner-take-all battle in Game 7 at Boston Garden. The Celtics had never lost a Game 7 in a playoff series, at home or on the road, but the Knicks were surprisingly confident. "I just never had any doubts we'd win, and I'm not that way," said New York coach Red Holzman. The Knicks fell behind early on but used a stifling pressure defense to key a 94–78 victory and continue their championship run.

"HE'S LIKE A BIRD. HE SWOOPS TOWARD THE BASKET AND SEEMS TO BE DESCENDING. THEN, AT THE LAST INSTANT, HE ELEVATES, AND YOU'LL SEE AN INCREDIBLE MOVE."

— COACH HUBIE BROWN ON BERNARD KING

years, New York quickly sank in the standings.

But there was a silver lining to the Knicks' dark cloud of bad luck. Thanks to its low finish in 1984–85, New York was entered in the first NBA Draft lottery. The lottery is a drawing to see which team gets the number-one overall pick, and in 1985, the prize was seven-foot center Patrick Ewing. The Knicks' name was drawn, and Ewing became the heart of the team for 15 years.

An outstanding defender and scorer at Georgetown University, Ewing had led the Hoyas to three college national championship games, and the Knicks were counting on the seven-footer to take them to glory as well. Ewing was a dominant presence in the paint and boasted a deadly fadeaway jump shot. He also had a brooding "game face" that intimidated opponents. Still, the "Ewing Era" got off to a rocky start. It took several years—and several coaching changes—before the Knicks were able to surround their powerful center with the right supporting players. This talented lineup included point guard Mark Jackson,

bruising forwards Charles Oakley and Anthony Mason, and guards John Starks and Gerald Wilkins. Together, they helped New York reel off a string of playoff appearances that started with the 1987–88 season and continued throughout the 1990s.

Before the 1991–92 season, the Knicks also added a new coach—the legendary Pat Riley, who had guided the Lakers to four NBA championships during the 1980s. Riley stressed a physical style of play, and the Knicks quickly developed a reputation for toughness. Opposing players often feared for their safety when they drove toward the basket. Riley's Knicks finished near the top of the NBA standings each of his four years in New York, reaching the Eastern Conference finals twice and the NBA Finals once in search of another title.

The Knicks came closest to that goal in the 1994 NBA Finals, when they grabbed a three-games-to-two lead over the Houston Rockets and needed just one more victory to claim the crown. It never came. Cold outside shooting, primarily by Starks, and the Knicks' failure to get the ball inside to Ewing in the crunch led to two heartbreaking defeats in Houston.

WALT FRAZIER

**POSITION GUARD
HEIGHT 6-FOOT-4
KNICKS SEASONS
1967-77**

Walt Frazier became a legend in New York for his style both on the basketball court and off it. Frazier was nicknamed "Clyde" by his teammates, after Warren Beatty's stylish character in the movie *Bonnie and Clyde*. When he wasn't thrilling fans in Madison Square Garden, Frazier loved being seen outside New York's poshest clubs, driving his Rolls-Royce "Clyde-mobile" and wearing a long fur coat and floppy fedora hat. A seven-time NBA All-Star, Frazier was nearly as exciting to watch when he played defense as when he was scoring or handing out assists on offense. Quick hands, catlike reflexes, and great court awareness helped Frazier earn a spot on the NBA's All-Defensive squad 7 times in his 10 seasons in New York. He was inducted into the Basketball Hall of Fame in 1987. Following his playing career, Frazier joined the Knicks' radio and television broadcast teams, where his love of big words and colorful rhymes—such as "dishing and swishing," "hustle and muscle," or "flexing and vexing"—earned him a new set of fans.

TIME TO REBUILD

SHARPSHOOTER ALLAN HOUSTON GAINED FAME FOR HIS 1999 PLAYOFFS BUZZER-BEATER.

Riley left New York in June 1995 to take over as coach of the Miami Heat and was eventually replaced by his longtime assistant, Jeff Van Gundy. New general manager Ernie Grunfeld rebuilt the club's roster before the 1996–97 season, bringing in forwards Larry Johnson and Buck Williams and guards Allan Houston and Chris Childs to surround Ewing. Guard/forward Latrell Sprewell and highflying center Marcus Camby were later added to the team's mix.

This new cast put together an amazing run in the 1999 playoffs. In the first round, New York shocked the top-seeded Heat on a last-second basket by Houston, clinching a win in the deciding Game 5. The Knicks then wiped out the Atlanta Hawks in the next round before challenging the Indiana Pacers in the Eastern Conference finals.

Things looked bleak when Ewing was lost to a season-

31

STARKS'S MONSTER DUNK

Madison Square Garden is known as "the world's most famous arena," and it's had many memorable moments in its history. One such moment is referred to simply as "The Dunk." During the 1993 playoffs against the rival Chicago Bulls, the undersized but bighearted guard John Starks brought the Garden crowd to its feet. With the Knicks holding a three-point lead and just a minute left in the game, Starks dribbled the ball up the court and made a quick move around a defender on a pick-and-roll play with teammate Patrick Ewing. The 6-foot-3 Starks drove the baseline, leaped up from outside the paint, and made a left-handed jam over Bulls tough-guy forward Horace Grant, with the great Michael Jordan coming in late to defend. Today, a display case in Madison Square Garden features Starks's dunk as one of the building's top 10 defining moments. Once, when asked how often the play comes up in conversation, Starks said, "Every day. Every day since it happened, people have been talking about that particular play. It was a very special play, no getting around it."

JOHN STARKS

LATRELL SPREWELL LED ALL SCORERS IN THE 1999 NBA PLAYOFFS WITH 407 TOTAL POINTS.

ending injury in the second game against Indiana. But the Knicks rallied, just as they had done in 1970 when Willis Reed went down. Johnson completed a miraculous, game-winning, four-point play at the end of Game 3, and the Knicks rode that momentum to defeat the Pacers in six games. Unfortunately, New York's magical run halted in the NBA Finals when the San Antonio Spurs proved too powerful for the undermanned Knicks.

A conference finals defeat in the 2000 playoffs convinced Knicks management that it was time to shake things up by trading away Ewing. The center's departure after 15 years in New York was an emotional one. "Patrick is a champion, even if he hasn't won a championship yet," said Coach Van Gundy. "He practiced and played like a champion each day he was here." With Ewing gone to the Seattle SuperSonics, the Knicks "went small," implementing a new offense based on the outside shooting and inside slashing of Houston, Sprewell, and Camby. The team scratched its way into the playoffs for the 14th consecutive year but fell quickly to the Toronto Raptors in the first round.

When the Knicks got off to a shaky 10–9 start in 2001–02, Coach Van Gundy suddenly resigned, and the team seemed to fall apart,

BERNARD KING

POSITION FORWARD
HEIGHT 6-FOOT-7
KNICKS SEASONS
1982–87

Bernard King spent nearly half of his Knicks career on the sidelines, rebuilding a shattered knee suffered late in January 1985. But when he was on the court, King was one of the most exciting offensive talents ever to wear a Knicks uniform. A two-time All-Star while in New York, King was nearly impossible to defend. In a 1984 first-round playoff series against the Detroit Pistons, he averaged more than 40 points per game despite having dislocated fingers on both hands and suffering from the flu. The key to King's success was his ability to slash by defenders for quick jumpers or spectacular dunks. "Bernard has an incredibly explosive first step to the basket," said his coach, Hubie Brown. King also had the uncanny ability to get his shot off while on the way up, before defenders could block it. King never stopped working, even when he was injured. He underwent two years of painful rehab, determined to continue his pro basketball career with the Knicks. When he walked on the court again late in the 1986–87 season, New York fans gave him a four-minute standing ovation.

finishing with a dismal 30–52 record. Following the season, management acted quickly and perhaps recklessly, trading Camby to the Denver Nuggets for All-Star center/forward Antonio McDyess, who had great talent but a long history of injuries. The gamble failed when McDyess hurt his knee during a preseason game and was lost for the entire year. Without a solid presence in the middle, the Knicks endured another sub-.500 campaign.

hat followed was a series of decisions that most New York basketball fans would look back on with horror. First, team president Scott Layden was fired by club owner James Dolan and replaced by Isiah Thomas, an outstanding former NBA player with only a mediocre record as a coach and administrator. But Dolan was sure that Thomas was a good choice. "Isiah is one of the most celebrated figures in the history of the NBA, and we believe he is the right person to lead this team into the future and deliver a championship-caliber team to all Knicks fans," Dolan said.

Thomas immediately began wheeling and dealing. First, he traded several players and draft picks to acquire point guard Stephon Marbury to lead the New York offense. The arrival of Marbury, a New York high school legend, excited local fans but made them anxious, too. Although he was an expert at breaking down opposing defenses with his quickness, Marbury had a reputation for being selfish, and fans questioned whether he would be able to jump-start the stalled Knicks offense and get the team back on the winning track.

Thomas brought in Hall of Fame coach Lenny Wilkens to run the club on the floor and followed with more player trades. Nearly the entire roster had changed over by season's end. Despite the chaos, Marbury pushed the Knicks into the 2004 playoffs with a 39–43 record, though they were quickly eliminated by the rival New Jersey Nets in the first round. Still, New York fans were optimistic about the team's chances of regaining its winning touch.

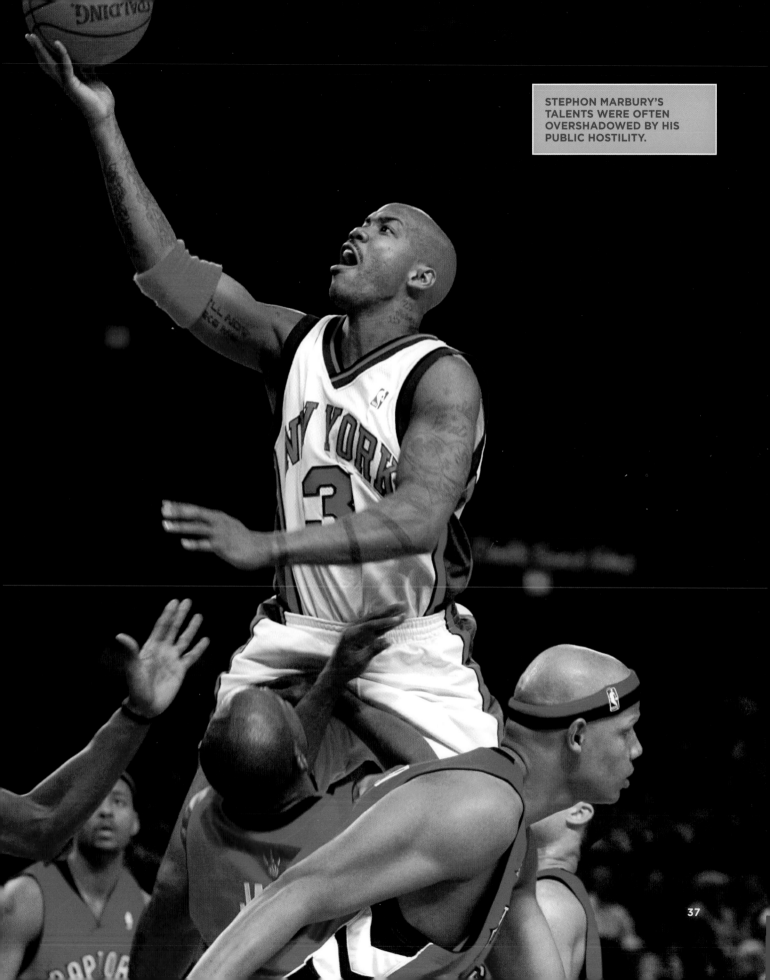

STEPHON MARBURY'S TALENTS WERE OFTEN OVERSHADOWED BY HIS PUBLIC HOSTILITY.

BACK TO THE PLAYOFFS

FORWARD AMAR'E STOUDEMIRE PROVIDED STAR POWER TO THE LACKLUSTER KNICKS.

The high hopes faded quickly. Thomas continued to tinker with the Knicks' roster over the next three seasons, but nothing seemed to work. He made some questionable trades for players such as center Eddy Curry, forward Zach Randolph, and guards Jamal Crawford and Steve Francis— all high-priced athletes whose long-term contracts caused the Knicks' payroll to exceed the league salary cap and restricted the team's ability to sign free agents. Thomas also fired Wilkens midway through the 2004–05 season and replaced him the following year with veteran coach Larry Brown. But the Knicks were mired in a losing cycle from which they couldn't seem to escape. Thomas and Brown quarreled openly throughout 2005–06, and Dolan was compelled to dismiss Brown, even though the coach had several years remaining on his expensive contract.

EDDY CURRY'S MID-CAREER HEALTH ISSUES LIMITED HIS POTENTIAL IN NEW YORK.

Dolan then insisted that Thomas himself coach the struggling team he had constructed and turn its fortunes around quickly if he wanted to keep his job.

When the Knicks got off to a slow start in 2006–07, chants of "Fire Isiah" began to resound in Madison Square Garden. Then Curry and Marbury keyed a mid-year winning streak, and Dolan decided to extend Thomas's contract despite the opposition of local fans and sportswriters. Thomas would last through one more disappointing season before he, too, was fired and replaced by Donnie Walsh as president and Mike D'Antoni as coach prior to the 2008–09 season.

The new team leaders had some key decisions to make about the club's style of play and its roster. D'Antoni, who had previously built the Phoenix Suns into a Western Conference "run-and-gun" powerhouse, wanted to establish an up-tempo offense in New York as well. "Our goal is to shoot within seven seconds or less," said D'Antoni, "to get a shot up before opponents can react." With that in mind, Walsh and D'Antoni replaced Marbury with former Chicago Bulls point guard Chris Duhon, a "pass-first, shoot-later" guard. They also decided to bench Curry and trade away several slower players for speedy forward Al Harrington and shooting guard Larry Hughes.

The team's increased hustle and enthusiasm attracted New York basketball fans back to the arena, where cheers replaced the boos of previous seasons, but the team still finished 2008–09 and 2009–10 with losing marks. As the next season began, the Knicks made some huge moves. First, they signed All-Star power forward Amar'e Stoudemire away from the Phoenix

PATRICK EWING

**POSITION CENTER
HEIGHT 7 FEET
KNICKS SEASONS
1985–2000**

Patrick Ewing was fortunate to have strong, broad shoulders, because for nearly 15 years, the 7-foot center had to carry the Knicks franchise on his back. From the time he was selected as the number-one overall pick in the 1985 NBA Draft, Ewing was expected to guide the Knicks back to championship glory. Most of those years, he was asked to lead the team to victory with only a mediocre supporting cast. Still, he continued to score, rebound, and block shots at a team-record pace. And he helped turn the franchise into one of the most competitive and financially successful teams in the league. Before Ewing arrived on the scene, the Knicks seldom filled the seats in Madison Square Garden. But the big man's presence revived New Yorkers' interest in pro basketball, and the team performed before standing-room-only crowds every home game for nine straight seasons. The Knicks won more than 71 percent of those contests, too. In February 2003, Ewing's number 33 jersey was retired by the Knicks. Five years later, he was inducted into the Basketball Hall of Fame.

HEAD COACH MIKE D'ANTONI'S FAST-PACED STRATEGY WORKED WELL FOR CHRIS DUHON.

LINSANITY TAKES HOLD

Undrafted and cut twice in the 2011–12 season, Jeremy Lin, a former Harvard University guard, appeared to be just a backup at the end of the Knicks' bench by the time he arrived in New York. Then, suddenly, it seemed as though everybody in New York City was wearing one of Lin's number 17 jerseys. "Linsanity" had begun. Over a six-week stretch, Lin was the toast of old New York. In early February, when other players were injured, Lin was promoted to starter and scored 38 points in a victory over guard Kobe Bryant and the Los Angeles Lakers. Lin hit a game-winning basket against the Toronto Raptors, and he passed out 14 assists against the defending-champion Dallas Mavericks. During a stretch in which the Knicks went 8–1, Lin averaged 25 points, 9.2 assists, 3.8 rebounds, and 2.2 steals per game. He scored 109 points in his first 4 starts, the most ever by any player in his first 4 starts in nearly 40 years. Stunningly, the Knicks did not re-sign Lin in the off-season, and the phenom agreed to a 3-year, $25.1-million deal to go to the Houston Rockets.

Suns for 5 years and $100 million. Then, midway through the season, they made a blockbuster trade with the Nuggets for superstar forward Carmelo Anthony.

Those moves paid off as New York went 42–40, its first winning record in a decade, and made the playoffs for the first time since 2004. Despite a 42-point, 17-rebound, 6-assist performance by Anthony in Game 2 of the first round, the Knicks were swept in 4 games by the Boston Celtics.

I n 2011–12, the Knicks again made the playoffs, but it proved to be an up-and-down season. They traded for 7-foot-1 center Tyson Chandler, who would be named the NBA's Defensive Player of the Year, and saw the emergence of exciting point guard Jeremy Lin. But after an 18–24 start to the lockout-shortened year, D'Antoni resigned. Under new coach Mike Woodson, the Knicks went 18–6 to close out the regular season before being bounced from the playoffs in five games by the eventual champion Heat. However, the Knicks' one win in the series was their first playoff victory since 2001. "I think it's the first of many," Stoudemire said. "Tonight was a great win for us, for our fans to finally get over that hump of those consecutive games we lost, I guess the Knicks, lost over those years in the playoffs."

Stoudemire was right. The next season, Anthony led the NBA with 28.7 points per game, and the Knicks went 54–28 to win the Eastern Conference's Atlantic Division. They defeated the Celtics in six games in the first round of the playoffs to win their first playoff series since 2000 but fell to the Pacers in the second round. Former NBA player-turned-analyst Jalen Rose

commented, "They don't get points in the paint, they don't make each other better, and they don't compete defensively for long periods of time. All things you need to do to win in the playoffs." As the aging Knicks roster faced the future, they would have to address such perceived shortcomings.

The Knicks continued to flounder in 2013–14, even as Anthony racked up big numbers that included a franchise-best record of 62 points in a January victory over the Charlotte Bobcats. Then a midseason front-office restructuring seemed to promise a major turnaround. Former player Phil Jackson, who had coached the Bulls and Lakers to a combined 11 NBA titles, was named team president. Fans and players alike believed the legendary coach's arrival would breathe new life into the Knicks. "There's energy in the city," said Woodson, who knew the team had a lot of work ahead. "We've dug a hole, and we're trying to dig our way out."

For more than 60 years, the New York Knicks have known how to put on a good show. New York fans who witnessed the valiant efforts of Willis Reed in the 1970s, the power of Patrick Ewing in the 1990s, and the flair of Carmelo Anthony in more recent years have come to expect dramatic and excellent performances in Madison Square Garden. And they hope that someday one of those shows will end with another NBA championship.

47

INDEX